AF094879

This Handwriting Notebook
Belongs To:

A

A is For

B

B is For

C

C is For

D

D is For

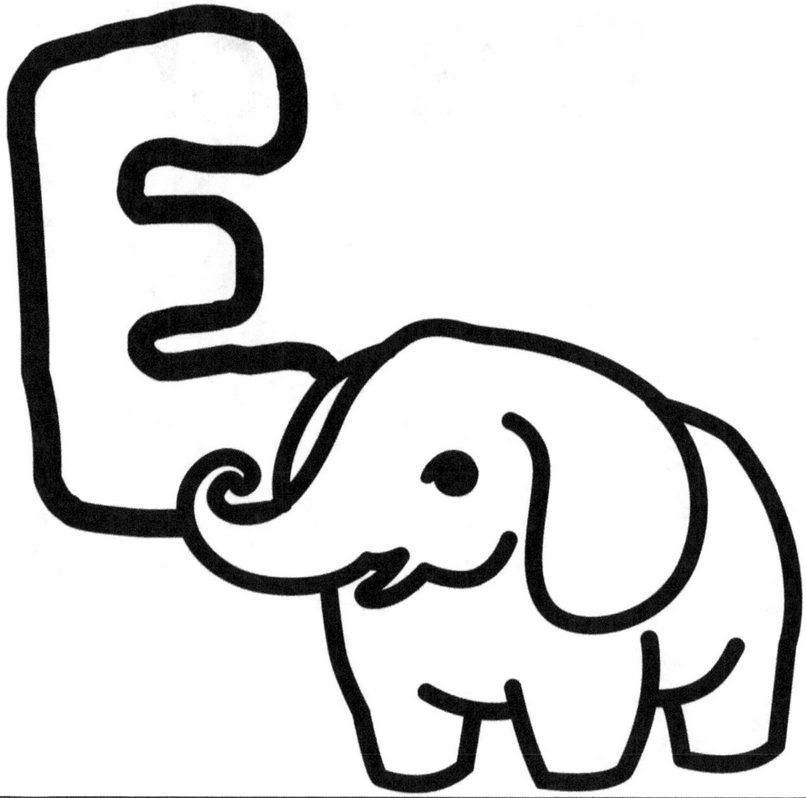

E is For

F

F is For

G

G is For

H

H is For

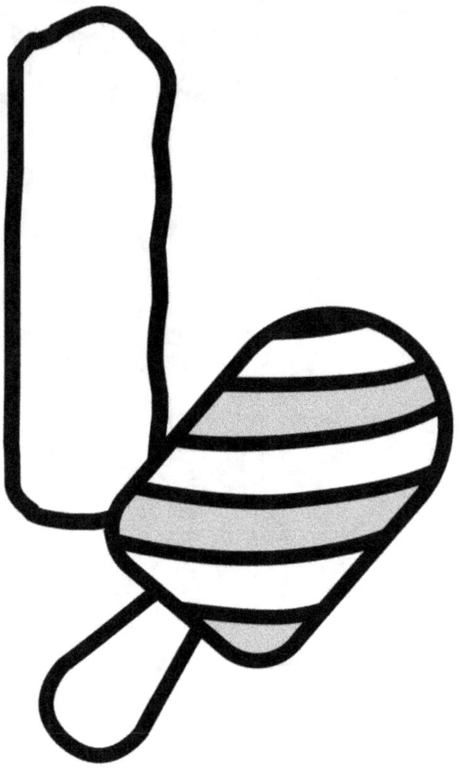

I

I is For

J

J is For

K

K is For

L is For

M

M is For

N

N is For

o

O is For

P

P is For

Q

Q is For

R

R is For

S

S is For

T is For

u

U is For

v

V is For

W

W is For

X

X is For

Y

Y is For

Z

Z is For

www.ingramcontent.com/pod-product-compliance
Lightning Source LLC
LaVergne TN
LVHW060325080526
838202LV00053B/4418
* 9 7 8 3 7 4 9 7 3 8 2 9 8 *